The Only House on the Left

The Only House on the Left

Poems by

W. Scott Hanna

© 2025 W. Scott Hanna. All rights reserved.
This material may not be reproduced in any form, published,
reprinted, recorded, performed, broadcast,
rewritten or redistributed without
the explicit permission of W. Scott Hanna.
All such actions are strictly prohibited by law.

Cover design by Shay Culligan
Cover image by Kathryn Weir
Author photo by Lauren Florence

ISBN: 978-1-63980-844-1

Kelsay Books
502 South 1040 East, A-119
American Fork, Utah 84003
Kelsaybooks.com

for Dad

Even at the very end, we were still laughing.

Acknowledgments

Thank you to the editors of the following journals and anthologies where many of these pieces first appeared:

Belt Magazine: "Still Life, Ohio Valley"

Change 7: "When Your Father Is Dying"

Cleaver Magazine: "Little Blue Box"

Fourth and Sycamore: "A Blossom," "New Orleans from Here," "A Winter of First Wanting"

Heartwood Literary Magazine: "River Song"

I Though I Heard a Cardinal Sing: Ohio's Appalachian Voices: "Cardinal"

Pine Mountain Sand and Gravel: "Directional," "All We Live Through," "Afterward," "Homecoming," "Drop-off and Pickup," "When the Sea Made Sense," "Ye Olde Alpha"

Porter House Review: "Years of Gravity"

Riparian: An Anthology of Ohio River Writing: "In Response to Your Responses"

Sheila-Na-Gig: "Grackle"

Still: The Journal: "The Unfolding," "Whiskey and the Universe," "Van Gogh's Sky," "The Only House on the Left"

Tributaria: Poetry, Prose, and Art Inspired by the Tributaries of the Ohio River Watershed: "Finally, Ohio"

I extend the utmost gratitude to the late, great, Dr. Jack Hattman, who gave me the confidence and inspiration to become a writer, to Dr. David J. Thomas, my first and best poetry teacher ever, and to the following poets and writers who, each in different ways, have provided mentorship, friendship, and inspiration—Richard Hague, Pauletta Hansel, Sherry Cook-Stanforth, C.J. Farnsworth, Daniel Flatley, and Marc Harshman.

Thank you to my family—extended and immediate—especially Mom, Dad, Sis, and Bro, for their undying love, support, and encouragement. Thank you to my wife, Shaye; my son, Roby; and my daughter, Emmy, without whom I would be lost.

Contents

Prologue: Years of Gravity   13

I.

The Only House on the Left   19
River Song   21
Life As If   22
When the Sea Made Sense   23
Birdsongs   25
Cardinal   27
Grackle   28
A Symphony (of Starlings)   30
The Long-Dead   32
Lucky Strikes, Unfiltered   34
Stringing the Rope   36
The McKinley High Annual   38
October, Canton, Ohio, 1948   40
Still Life, Ohio Valley   43

II.

The Parable of the Boy and the Mountain   47

III.

To Unfold   59
In Response to Your Responses   61

Ye Olde Alpha	63
New Orleans from Here	65
The Answer to Why	67
Between Times	69
Reconciliation	70
Directional	72
All We Live Through	74
Not the Same Red	75
A Winter of First Wanting	78

IV.

Waiting for My Son	83
The Unfolding	87
Drop-Off and Pickup	89
Van Gogh's Sky	93
Full Count	95
Little Blue Box	97
Someone Else's Blood	101
A Blossom	106
Whiskey and the Universe	108
Still Alive, Still Signing	110
March Morning, 2020	114
Father-Daughter Discussion	116
Finally, Ohio	121
Inventory	123
Iron Man	125

V.

Conversation at Dawn	129
Now, You Are	131
When Your Father Is Dying	134
Afterward	137
Leaving Home	138
Rt. 7 Confession	140
Winter Solstice Eve Morning	143
Valley Pastoral: The View from Table Rock Lane, Election Day, 2024	145
Daylight Savings Morning	146
Stars Without Stories	148
What We Have Left	150
Homecoming	152

Prologue: Years of Gravity

My father falls back against me with the full weight of eighty-two years, and I remember this:

The water is icy cold. Without knowing the science of gravity, I understand the physics of sinking, knowing the water alone will not hold me up, knowing my arms and legs have to work to keep my head above the water, knowing my father will eventually let me go.

I push back with all my strength to load him from the motorized wheelchair into the car, the weight of the memory of each year pressing into my side. I struggle to gain leverage and lift him, one arm under the back of his knees (which have not worked for decades), the other under his back, as a groom carries a bride over a threshold. His years are so heavy, so saturated with pain and regret.

He holds me in the water. I can't be more than five or six. The backyard pool is draped in summer sun, light pouring down and dancing, bending and shimmering on the sky-blue pool bottom. He holds me there, waiting to let go, feeling my fear, my tension.

I am thinking about now and then, and at the same time, trying to keep my father from falling, to avoid a 911 call for the third time in two weeks, not including the times my mother never tells me about.

I watch the way the light dances in the underwater sky. I am safe with his hands around my waist, but I know he is going to let go. I am afraid. This is my first real lesson about gravity—even in water, the earth still pulls us down.

Past and present turn on a constant loop. I am straining with all my strength to hold him up, remembering how he held me safe then.

Neither of us wants to accept what is happening, all the strength I can bare pushing back against the weight of his whole life. It's too much, the memory of each lost year pressing into my side, pinning my leg against the open car door, blood starting down my shin. I am holding on with everything.

He lets go and I am screaming, kicking and flailing and splashing, trying to stay afloat, suspended between two skies, not ready to be alone, not ready at all to be let go. I am sinking, water converging to cover my mouth, chlorine stinging my nose. I close my eyes, waiting for my father's hands to save me.

I don't want him to remember only now, or all the falls the past year, or the ambulance ride two weeks from now that will take him away forever from the house he has lived in for forty-eight years, where he built his life, made our lives as perfect as he knew how. I don't want him to remember any of this, his one leg in the car, his other with foot planted on the street, no strength left to move his own legs, my straining to hold him up.

I am pulling myself through the blue water, learning so quickly the way legs and arms use water to resist gravity. I remember my head resurfacing, my father now at the shallow end, empty arms beckoning me to swim back to him all on my own. And I am kicking and paddling all alone, my mother and brother and sister on the pool deck cheering me on.

I gather all my strength to try to hoist him up, to keep him from sliding off the passenger seat into the street. Certain things we just don't want to know about until they're real, to admit that a time comes when the only good parts left are all in the past, a time when we can no longer tread water, no longer put food to our own lips, no longer hobble to the bathroom on our own, no longer hold ourselves upright, no longer get into a car unassisted, no longer do any of the things that living requires without the need of someone else's hands, without the need for someone to hold us up.

For the first time all by myself, I swim from the deep end back into my father's arms. He picks me up and lifts me high above his head in celebration. We are smiling and laughing in the water, in the sun, under a bright blue sky, in the untouchable past.

I.

Suddenly I realize
That if I stepped out of my body I would break
Into blossom.

~James Wright

The Only House on the Left

Forty years before
this brokenness,
before bed-riddenness
exchanged longing
for servitude,
before the silent midsummers on porches,
where you became monuments,
to time's slowing and speeding,
and the coming on of that evening
light in august,
before knowing all that its passing
will take away,
the crabapple bloomed
white the spring of '74,
forsythia bursting
yellow on the hill,
green ground and wood
tugging at our guts even then,
pulling down,
swelling and pregnant,
memory digging in,
root, and leaf, and sky, turning
toward words
we would never end up saying,
always turning toward
the empty winter of now,
when cardinals croon in the pines,
chickadees burrow in the yews,
bare-branched maple and locust thatch
against gray November dream skies
and the light in the back woods,

falls finally in morning,
silvering the frosted grass,
and later in evening,
lays the pine shadows out
long across the east field
by the empty house
where no eyes, no voice, no body,
not even memory
is left to bear witness.

River Song

Four miles above
the valley of the Ohio,
from the sliding waters,
from silent currents,
from the barge wake
lapping the shore,
I lie in bed. I am ten,
in the front bedroom
of the only house on the left,
caught somewhere between
sleeping and waking.

Somehow, only in winter,
the sound of the river,
the low bellow of horn blasts,
travels clear as ice on clean cold wind,
through the hollows,
the barren tangled trees,
and flows up over Table Rock ridge,
enwraps the haunted steeple
of Lawrencefield Chapel,
pours down again into the dale,
and finally climbs the south slope,
settles in the starry dark
behind my closed eyes,
where I watch its waves roll
over the hills, traverse the full
four miles from the valley,
somewhere between
sleeping and waking—
the song of the river
in midwinter.

Life As If

I am six, I am pure, I am invincible,
I am holding on to my father

until the world slows its motion to nearly stopping,
branch filtered sunlight crossing shadows twisting

along Long Run toward home lulling me off to sleep,
tiny grip slackening from his sides when he leans

the motorcycle into the last sharp bend toward home
at forty miles per hour, and in that second

my entire life becomes an 'if,' suspended, pulling out,
centrifuging, then tumbling to its end in a roadside ditch.

The next day in kindergarten the boys and girls
pause over my tiny, empty desk-chair

to wonder for a moment why I am not there
and then continue on building block-castles,

finger painting new galaxies, proceeding to the next letter
to build words in a language I will never know

in a life I will never live long enough to become
scarred, to become fragile, to become broken

to be holding on, fifty years later,
to my father, still, to hear his voice

reaching into my dream-deep sleep,
calling me back to the living.

When the Sea Made Sense

Over the night sounds
      consuming the back woods,
           cicadas chorusing through the screen,
in a full voice, measured,
      young and strong,
           embodied in the master bedroom
of the only house on the left,
      my father reads to me.

In a pool of lamp light
      the book lies open,
           yellowed, brittle pages,
faded black pen scrawls
      all through the margins of *Hamlet*.

Trying to hide his sudden weeping
      beneath something beyond
           the real pain he does not yet know,
something beyond fear and failure,
      beyond even his own son,
           who sits listening,
absorbing every letter
      shaped to sound
           shaped into words,
unearthing the buried heart
      of a young father,
           his voice now trembles on through the rest
                of the silence, reading,

      Now cracks a noble heart. Good night, sweet prince.
      And flights of angels sing thee to thy rest.

This had to be
        the moment
                when the sea
                        finally made sense,
the way the tide
        out of which we crawled
                      never stops moving,
the illusion
        of the morning sun rising
                up into what
                        we used to believe
                              was heaven.

Birdsongs

Second of all
the sounds

in my memory
of all the sounds

at the only house on the left
are the songs

of the chickadee, nuthatch,
finch, waxwing,

cardinal, grackle,
jay, grosbeak,

each note's call
and response filling

some ancient space
echoing the west

woods' silence.

*

First of all
the sounds

in my memory
of all the sounds

at the only house on the left,
way up on the southern hilltop

rising above
the oak and apple

and sumac and Osage
and locust and spruce—

my mother's voice
calling,

for fifty years now,
on the wind

at dusk.

Cardinal

I know my mother's weeping is real by the way
she exhales, fragmented and flailing,

like someone newly mourning. Head only hip-high,
I stare up to her saddened face, too young to understand

any of this, but old enough to know something
is broken, and that with breaking, anguish follows,

old enough to know she would want to see
the male cardinal, newly perched in the bare maple

just outside the back window. I nearly tell her
to look, to watch its bright red flame up

against all that winter. But I keep quiet
and listen, try to hear in place of her grief,

the cardinal's song just beyond the glass.

Grackle

Our mother told us it was okay to kill
when we were boys in summer

no other birds but the grackles
that would gather and cackle

in the trees behind the only house on the left
because they poached nests and stole food

from the innocent wren or robin, so it was okay
to aim and fire a pellet gun at a living thing,

to end a life deliberately,
to turn something living dead.

We could hear their awful cackle and squawk
high in the locusts in the woods behind the house,

nothing like the melody of cardinal or finch
or the occasional bluebird or grosbeak

who would all scatter from the feeders
as a grackle approached to then eat its glut,

so we hunted for their purple heads,
shiny and glistening even against a gray March sky,

until one summer day we picked one off from a branch,
and it fell to the ground, flopped and flapped until dead.

My big brother carried our kill to a rock in the woods
and, as if a post-mortem punishment for poaching,

dropped a ten-pound rock on its splayed body
again and again until the entrails spilled out

and I'd seen the insides of a life for the first time,
but even in the glob of guts on the rock

I could see its marble glass black eye still
staring skyward into a future of nothing,

its glossy purple head, so dark, so beautiful now,
and I felt for sure someone, or something,

there in the whispering wind through leaves,
with grave disappointment, witnessing.

A Symphony (of Starlings)

Thirteen billion years
      after the universe,

a hot, spinning mass
      the size of a human fist,
           in a blink
burst into being,

a single-minded symphony
      of starlings
feeds in the fescue and clover

      by a river
           men once named
beautiful, and

then

      in a sudden, furious
           explosion of flapping,

startles skyward
      into perfect unified flight

        up into

the now-open
      orange-red dusk,

rises from the valley,
        outward, toward space,

                upward expanding,

and marries with
        the measured inevitable

coming on

        of the stars.

The Long-Dead

I keep listening for the voices
of the long-dead,
down a hallway, in another room,
across the river, at the foot of a hill.
I want to believe
I can hear them.
I want to believe
they know I am
searching,
traveling placename by placename,
a litany that maps blood
across time and stone and water—
Ulster, Gloucester,
Massachusetts,
Pennsylvania, Ohio,
and leads finally here—

> Name: James Hanna
> Birthplace: Donegal, 1786
> Occupation: Farmer
> Deathplace: Steubenville, Ohio, 1846

So much more than numbers and names
speak for the dead—
a patch of ground once stood upon,
dawn breaking over the hills,
harvest air, breathed in deep,
the labor up and down a river of new earth,
and finally the fruit,
harvested for all those
still yet to be living.

I want to believe
the dead can see me
digging through this shoebox,
shuffling through faded sermon notes,
hand-written genealogies,
daguerreotypes, disintegrating photographs,
scrolling through scanned census pages
for any clues at all.

How far back is far enough
until time circles here?

    Belmont, Ohio,
    beautiful mountain, great river.

I keep listening for the sounds
of the long-dead,
a voice, a name,
boots scraping the dirt,
echoes of a plow breaking
new-settled ground.

I want to believe
they can witness
I am.

Lucky Strikes, Unfiltered

for Susan Jane Hanna, 1917–1994

Bourbon and cigarettes and a history of stories
I was too young to know how to remember,

or to pay attention to, or to understand
why I even should, play back in memory,

vivid as her big flower-print blouses, bright yellow pants,
gaudy necklaces dangling with in-set turquoise,

medallion-sized earrings, and the swirling
of perfume and chlorine and smoke

during before dinner drinks at Point Breeze Drive
as Glenn Miller records spin on the stereo,

and then the after-dinner drinks,
followed by the after-after-dinner drinks,

and the big bands still play on louder
and louder, a backdrop soundtrack for old stories

spun about evenings driving out Rt. 88 to Breezy Heights,
all the late-night revelries with Fergy and Roe,

and Edgar "Headgear" Martin, told with the freshness
of yesterday, always ending with a crescendo of laughter.

Just beyond the screened porch, cross-legged
in the folding lawn chair she conducts the orchestra,

motioning out the 4/4 time of "A String of Pearls,"
waving a red-lipstick-stained Lucky Strike like a baton

as the needle drops on to "Smoke Gets in Your Eyes,"
and the notes from Miller's lead clarinet flitter like birds

out over the Brooke County hills, and with the hummingbirds
sipping red-dyed sugar water, red rose bushes in full bloom,

her beloved now home safe from the war,
she lights another cigarette, and to the scent

of grilling steaks and onions, to the jazz-backed
hills and hollows of this perfect Appalachian evening,

she raises another full glass of bourbon and Coke
and offers a silent melodic toast:

> *Here's to being alive, unfiltered, and beautiful.*
> *It all tastes so goddamned good.*

Stringing the Rope

    for William Herbert Hanna, 1915–1983

Gin and motor oil, stained glass and silence,
grease-creased hands and the buried memory

of Normandy I was too young to ask about
or know that I even should.

Working under the hood of a 1948 step-down Hudson
in the dark shadows of Tri-ad Motors,

cigarette pasted to lower lip, lost somewhere
in the wrenching and cranking of mechanisms,

your mind must have wandered back
to June 6th, 1944, and then maybe in the next moment

back to the day you strung the rope over the sycamore
branch to hang the old tire swing for us.

How everything must have felt different after
that homecoming, stepping off the ship

that brought you home, a stranger back in your native land,
your corner of Appalachia, the details sharpened and quickened,

the touch of your wife's hand, the weight
of your young son in your arms, the deep

hollows of Brooke County, the craggy
banks of Buffalo Creek, the water, smooth over stones,

clear and bloodless, and even thirty years later, the laughter
of your grandchildren swinging from the sycamore,

our faces nothing like your brothers' I imagine
you still must see in the blood on the shore,

not bleeding and gunned down and dying,
but laughing and swinging and alive.

The McKinley High Annual

    for Kathryn Augusta Robeson, 1909–1971

Only a yearbook photograph and the caption,
Her dress, her manners, all who saw, admired,

and maybe a picture or two from old slide reels,
sparse stories of dressing the part in her Sunday best,

or ritual appearances at church, more social obligation than faith,
demands of manners, piano practice, primness, properness,

and then the emptiness and blankness of an end without memory
are all I have been told of my grandmother's story.

I'd like to think that one midsummer day in 1942,
in Canton, Ohio, safe in a suburb from a world at war

and decades before her mind became a blank slate,
before the straight jacket and hospitals and restraints,

back when there was only youth and beauty and love,
her body was overtaken by the sway and rhythm of time,

the primal current that conducts one person to another,
maybe in late afternoon, or early evening,

the day's steady light sweeping on toward dusk,
she pulled her husband close,

all in the flurry and beating of hearts and time,
a consummation never meant to be

anything but connection, a moment of giving in
became a single moment of overwhelming longing

that set into motion the long unfurling transmission
of blood to blood to blood.

October, Canton, Ohio, 1948

for Royal D. Robeson, 1898–1973

Steady static humming flow
and rush of radio

crowd sounds crackle
over suburban streets,

a bat cracks, and a ball kicks by
third base and down the line,

as you're propped back on the porch
at 816 Colonial Boulevard,

your daughter at play in the front yard,
white dress, and little black dog,

while Jim Britt and Mel Allen
paint with rising voices,

a portrait of Lou Boudreau
turning a double play,

and your muscle memory
yearns and moves in synch:

the quick step, shoulder rotating
from the hips, the snap of ball on leather,

and you can still smell the dirt,
the chalk, the grass, still hear

the thousand murmuring voices
in the stands, rising to crescendo,

rising in the dust,
still remember rounding third

and heading home in the game that would
clinch the Western Conference Championship,

you and Grasshopper Dempsey, Ollie Klee,
and the rest of the Buckeyes

tying Michigan for the 1924 title,
but now it's twenty-four years after

you took the field with Hodge Workman
and the Miller Brothers, and you stare

into the twilight, listening as Eddie Robinson
singles to right driving in Ken Keltner

for the insurance run that clinches
the World Series for Cleveland,

with no vision of a future
in which your daughter,

only five in 1948, will bear a son
who would father a son who would

drive in three runs, score two, and close out
the game on the mound to win the 2025 OVAC

championship for St. Clairsville High School,
because right now, it's just October,

Canton, Ohio, during the time of radio,
the past nowhere near the present,

and you're just a father on a porch
with a daughter in the yard,

and a great-grandson who will
bear your name way out

in the far-off left field of a future
I wish you could have seen.

Still Life, Ohio Valley

In early morning the tributaries at Pittsburgh meld,
then flow on for centuries, cutting the valley
out of the earth, heavy with water, light with stone.

*

South southwest below the hills above Bridgeport, Ohio
blackbirds congregate in March by thousands,
lifting, lighting, lifting in sudden bursts
of black wings on a gray sky.

*

Upriver the black weight that held the hills
feeds the barge anchored below the towering coal tipple
just beyond Pike Island Dam.

*

Below North Tenth street what little remains
of the old tree house rots in the sun where
Ricky, Mike, Jay and I choked on the smoke
of our first cigarettes in the summer of '86,
raided river gardens of old men,
and sifted through the sad wreckage of the Ohio.

*

Off Highland Road at dusk black heaps rise from
the ripped gouge to hem the mirror-black surface
of the slurry that upturns in the sky the smokestacks
at Brilliant, and Follansbee into something almost beautiful.

*

Near Lower Twin Island, ghosts of poets loom upriver
from tenement campers where the hungry huddle around flames,
the living gather along with the dead to gaze into the currents,
or to wander the B&O right of way, looking for home
beyond the ruined bones of the city.

*

Out of the hills, out of the past and the dark damp woods,
from under the shadow of St. Joseph's Convent,
the cold waters of Long Run I trailed into the valley as a boy
cling still to the age-long secret of a murdered sister.

*

The valley in October glows orange and yellow
above the double-wides and gravel-dirt roads
of Meadowlands Trailer park where standing flood waters
from Short Creek reflect rust, laundry lines,
broken bicycles, crumpled trampolines,
fallen satellites, and failed pickups.

*

Just over the hill in Oakmont million-dollar men
recline in million-dollar homes.

*

All through the valley the heavy lives men have lived
and women have lived and children have lived
out the pain and suffering and weight of hundreds of years
of layers of dirt and rust to move everything, everyone,
to doubt and wonder whether the water still flowing by in the river
has anything left in it that might save them,
or whether it's even moving, or finally, after all this,
just standing still.

II.

*And the point is, to live everything. Live the questions now.
Perhaps you will then gradually, without noticing it,
live along some distant day into the answer.*

~Ranier Maria Rilke

The Parable of the Boy and the Mountain

1. And so the boy stood at the foot of a great and tall mountain, looking up to where it stretched into the sky, farther than he could see or even imagine, beyond clouds, beyond sunlight, beyond starlight, and he wondered what was up there, so he started to climb, and the farther he climbed, the steeper the mountain became, but he wanted to know, so he kept climbing, and this is what he found.

2. He came first upon a green wood of maple and pine and locust, and through the wood ran a street with four houses on one side and one house on the other, and there in the yard of the only house on the left lay sleeping a large brown and white dog.

And the boy woke the dog, and she looked up at him with dark and deep eyes, and from then on, she loved him with blind faith and followed him through all his imaginings in forests of trees and blue skies rolling, and they lay in pine shade together watching the clouds and the summers roll past.

But soon enough the dog grew old, became tired, and she could no longer follow him into the woods or into the hills, and it was harder and harder for her to stand, and one day she fell, and her eyes closed, her breath stopped, her heart stopped, and he buried her in the dirt of the mountain. He smoothed over the dirt and marked her spot, and he continued on up the mountain, and he felt a little heavier, but did not yet feel tired.

3. He climbed on until one day he arrived at a door that opened to a dark, dusty, narrow stairway that led to another door that opened into a great room, and he went inside, and there before a vast mirror he met a man who sat cross-legged, breathing in slow, out slow. For many days and many nights, the great man taught him how to breathe the air and to move in ways he'd never imagined—like tigers move and like eagles fly and like dragons spin and swirl.

And the man said to him, *What you have learned here will remain with you your entire life. Always remember that.* But, like the dog had to go, so too did the man have to go, so he said goodbye to the great man, and the boy felt like crying now but did not because he knew there was so much more to see and to do, and he left the temple and continued up the mountain, and the mountain grew a little steeper now, but still he did not grow tired.

4. Soon enough, he came to a beautiful young girl with long black hair braded in strands of motley-colored beads. She had wonderful bronze skin and wore a long flowy flowery dress and danced in music notes and summer.

And she let her dress fall to the ground and held out her arms and she led him to a threshold and beckoned him to come in, and he found himself lying on the floor of a dim room of a million colors he dared not even dream before. And music played and colors swirled, and his heart raced faster and faster . . .

But, like all people do, the girl had to go, and then the mountain grew ever steeper.

5.   But still he climbed and climbed and soon came to an old woman, large and smiley, who handed him a pen and a piece of paper, and she said to him, *Write what is in your heart. Write what you have found and lost.*

And he took the pen and paper and wrote without thinking about the house and woods and the dog who died and the girl in the million-colored room, and when he wrote he felt that all those things were there again but knew they were also gone away, and his insides filled with empty and hurt.

And when the old woman read the paper, she said, *You do this very well,* and that was the first time someone believed in him.

So, the woman gave him more paper and a pen to carry with him on up the mountain.

6. And he continued climbing, and now he felt slightly tired, and his head hurt just a little, and when he breathed, he breathed deeply, just like the man in the temple showed him, and he tasted the air high in the mountain, and that helped him to keep climbing on even though he felt a heaviness pulling down that he did not feel when he began.

7. Soon he arrived at a tall tower where he entered to find thousands and thousands of rows and rows of books. And when he read them, he thought some of them good and some of them bad.

Some made him laugh. Some made him cry. Some made him stare out windows in wonder. Some made him laugh and cry and wonder all at once.

Then he soon grew tired and left the tower of books and continued up the mountain, taking with him the books he thought were best, mostly the ones that made him laugh and cry and wonder all at once.

And now the mountain grew ever steeper and the weight to carry even heavier.

8. And soon he came to another beautiful young woman with blonde-brown hair and fair skin and deep soulful eyes.

And she said to him, *I love you.*

And he said to her, *I want to be inside you forever.*

And they became rainwater and wind and flickering candlelight, summer twilight, wet springtime grass, deep purple dawn, sea foam and swell, and they lay under open windows listening to the late evening far-off rolling of thunder.

All the weight for a moment lifted. And he lay there unburdened and stripped, his head on her chest, her arms around him, and in the rising and falling of her breath, he knew that she loved him, and he knew right then that he loved her, but also that a day would come when he would not.

So, he knew he had to leave, that there was more to see on up the mountain, and he began climbing again, but now the mountain was terribly steep, and his feet began to hurt, and his legs began to ache, and his insides grew empty and full of the heavy weight of everything that was once there.

9. He climbed on and at length came to a gathering of three erudite men.

The first was named William, tilted back in a porch chair, a bottle of whiskey in his right hand, a copy of Joyce in the other, and William said to him, *The past is not dead. It's not even past.*

And the second man sat cross-legged and naked and proud in the grass, and he said his name was Walt. And Walt said to him, *You are of old and young, of the foolish as much as the wise.*

And the third man was named William like the first, but he wore strange parti-colored clothes, and he wrote on parchment with a quill and held a skull in his hand, and William asked him, *What is this quintessence of dust?*

And all three men gave him many books, and he carried them with him along the way, with the books from the hall, and the pen and paper from the woman, and all the weight of everything, and he managed to carry all of it because he knew there was still so much more to come.

10. And the mountain was much steeper now, and he grew very tired, and he thought about turning back, and he began to wonder if all this were even worth it, because his head hurt more now, and his heart hurt too, and inside he was confused.

So, he looked up to where the mountain stretched into the sky farther than he could see or even imagine, beyond clouds, beyond sunlight and starlight, and he wondered what was up there, and even though he knew many things now, he also knew that there had to be so much more because he could still feel so much empty in his heart, and so he kept climbing.

11. Then miles later, he came to a circle of friends who passed from each to each a small pipe.

And they offered him the pipe and he breathed in the smoke of pipe and his legs felt heavy and his arms felt heavy and his legs felt light and his arms felt light and everything slowed down and lifted and floated and floated away . . .

Then he left the friends and continued up the mountain, and the mountain grew steeper with every step, but still he kept climbing and climbing and searching for more, but for what he did not know.

12. Soon enough he came to a baby girl, and the baby looked at him and smiled and gurgled and cooed, and he picked the child up, and he held it close to his heart and felt the child breathing and living.

He set the child down to sleep and watched her, and way inside where no one could see, he cried for her, knowing that one day she too will have to climb and climb and climb and gain and lose and hurt, and he felt so sad for the little girl but happy also because at last he was beginning to understand, and soon he felt he that had strength to go on.

So, he continued up the mountain, and the mountain was even steeper, so steep he had to use his hands to claw the earth and pull himself up.

13. At last, he came to a doorway marked *schoolhouse* and felt he had climbed enough, read enough, felt and lost and hurt enough to go in, and so he went, and there he stood at the head of a room of many young students.

And he told them about the white and brown dog he lost, and the man in the temple and what he had learned there, about the flower girl, and about the large woman who made him write, about the beautiful girl by the ocean at dawn, and even about the circle of friends and the smoke from the pipe. And he told them about the baby girl who smiled and cooed and filled part of his empty heart. And he told them about the three men, and the tower of books, and he even gave them some of the books to read, and he even showed them some of the things he had written on the way up the mountain.

And he said to them, *Read these books; they will fill parts of you that you did not know were empty.*

And some of them read, but some of them did not.

To those who followed him, he said, *Your mountain has now become steeper.*

And to those who did not, he said, *You must find your mountain and begin climbing.*

And some of them began climbing, but some of them did not.

Soon enough he knew he had to move on, as all people do, and he left the schoolhouse and continued up the mountain.

14. But now he had grown into loss and pain and memory and love, and the mountain grew steeper and steeper and steeper, until soon he was climbing straight up, and his legs began to hurt, and his arms began to

hurt, and his heart began to swell, and his hands began to bleed from the clawing and scratching and grasping, and soon enough he had to let go.

And when he let go, he fell down and down, and as he fell, everything he had done and seen on his way up the mountain flashed by in a flurried blur and melding of color and light—all the students, the old men, the golden temple, the hall of books, the beautiful girls, the infant child.

And he fell and fell and fell and fell until he found himself, broken, bloodied, and half-buried, at the bottom of a great big mountain, where its foot met the waters of a river, and now he saw not one mountain, but another, and another, and another, and he set his head upon the ground, closed his eyes and slept.

15. And when he awoke on the river bank, he knew, knew all the names of the birds, and trees, and small towns along the river, and he even knew the mountains were called *Appalachia* and the river was called *Ohio,* and so he bathed in the river's waters and gathered the mountains in his arms, washed the blood from his face, stood, felt his feet root in the ground, looked downriver where water flowed around a bend farther than he could see or even imagine, and he wondered what was there where the water flowed out of sight.

So, he started walking until at last he stood again at the foot of a great and tall mountain, looking up to where it stretched into the sky, farther than he could see or even imagine, beyond clouds, beyond sunlight and starlight. And he knew that whatever he found on the way would first be, and then eventually not be, and that the weight in his heart was both joy and sorrow, emptiness and abundance, and so he started to climb, and the farther he climbed, the steeper the mountain became. But he knew now, the pain of it all would be worth everything, the beauty and the sadness of the having and the losing, falling again and again with the weight of a full heart.

III.

*I give you my blank heart.
Please write on it
what you wish.*

~Li-Young Lee

To Unfold

like water
        over stone
this page
      a letter
            a word

a seed
      into the coarse
            hands of time

as a new life
      a new idea
           born

into the universe
      or two
           or three
                or a number
                      unknowable

into the falling
      of a blossom
           pink
              or white
                  or any shade
                      of being
into this line
      of this version
           of this verse

```
into the present
            time forward
                        past
                                time backward
unfolded
      into the middle
                  of our coupling

this cosmos
        this time
                this light

unfolded
      onto this page
                        and the next . . .
```

In Response to Your Responses

for Dave Thomas and James Wright

You were both there, still,
when I stood, fallen and broken-winged
on the banks of the Ohio
just behind Wheeling Spring
in early April.

And you remain there, still,
every time I drive alone
through South Wheeling,
grieving sullen recollections
of a three-month sentence in hell,
reliving the one evening
when I escaped the Eoff Street apartment,
where circle-curls of cigarette smoke
enwreathed whispers of suicides
and swirled about the faces
of all the fallen and dry-winged women,
their memories, their pasts
now woven into my own.

Just west of Water Street
I stood, gazing,
into glassy Ohio currents—
a black night-mirror—
searching for the soul
I knew I never would find, nor even had,
pondering the water,
a grave to so many.

But now I think maybe here,
you were right, Jim (Can I call you "Jim"?),
just south and across the river
from Bridgeport, Ohio,
all three of us somehow rose
out of this infected hell,

resurrected, if only,
by the promise
of the next blank page.

Ye Olde Alpha

for Bill and Jay

You could love here . . .
              ~Richard Hugo

Below the beady-eyed expressions of antelope,
the mounted deer head in the corner that stares glass-eyed

across the room to the six-foot span of moose antlers
as wide as four bar stools, a guy could love here,

where time comes to a halt, no windows, no light
but for the smoke-filmed yellowed ceiling track,

the time of day told only by changing faces of bartenders
and the long, colorless, worn expressions

of two or three regulars, slouching over longnecks,
eyes bent toward the Keno screen, or gazing blankly

at the television in the corner, or into nothing at all,
and all the while, no matter the kind of night, day, season,

dozens of taxidermized animal heads hang in the yellow-dim haze,
gazing over us, who stand wall-flowered and checked by fear,

those immortalized expressions, glassy-eyed and terrified,
the only witnesses to the almost one-night fucks that never were.

The indignant deer, head and feet trophied
above the bar, seems to gesture out,

with its two severed, mounted, and upturned hooves,
a double fuck you to us all.

If we drink long enough into delirium, we can feel
their eyes moving, watching, waiting.

So many nights we spent here enwombed
from the outside, cocooned from whatever was out there

that we were too afraid to go back into,
Irish car bombing and shooting Drambuie and pool until last call,

like the one July night when we defied the passage of time,
and once Milly kicked us out into the street,

not too proud, but too stupid to go home,
we retrieved a box of Coors Light cans

and returned well after 3 a.m. to sit on the stoop
below the switched-off neon lounge sign,

and there we toasted with lukewarm beer,
pondering where we were going or where we even were,

between earth and city, country and lights,
Carmel Road, Wheeling, WV, and the rest of the world,

all the while inside, the animal eyes stared still, and the giant moose
antlers spread out in the dark like an angel's wings.

New Orleans from Here

Having lingered half-sober about cobbled streets
through October evenings behind Jackson Square,

drifted with the notes of a solitary trumpet
in the gas-lamp light well past midnight,

stood on the front stoop of the Faulkner house
where echoes of a past that's not even past

beckon before I even arrive home
to my dying valley's labor and sweat and pain

breaking under the molten orange glow
that once fired the Ohio, smoldering still

just enough to shadow the silent street corners
at night where there is no music but the distant thrums

of a cover band playing "Country Roads" for the thousandth time
and maybe, the solitary pedaling of Moondog up Main Street,

from the side of the silent bronze Mingo Indian
keeping failed watch over Wheeling Hill, I descend

toward the river, pass under the darkened, blank marquis
of the Capitol Theater, to the bank just below

the Fort Henry Bridge and slip into the quiet
chemical currents of the Ohio, down south

and west and further on into the Mississippi,
on down to the wide banks at New Orleans

where pools of yellow and blue light gather
on Royal Street at dusk, and a block or two over

on Dauphine where no one has ever heard
nor even knows the chords to "Country Roads,"

a crowd dances around the deep plunk of the bass,
the crooning sax and trumpet, the notes drifting

up and out over the street, the square,
and on upriver, calling to me somewhere way inside,

this is the place you belong.

The Answer to Why

Because the moon's light
draped across the room,

and you unbuttoned your jacket,
slipped off your shoes,

and my worn face rested
on the bare warm skin of your chest,

and your voice sang soft
filling time's hollow wandering,

and we exhaled and inhaled
atoms and dust and light

in the almost-empty room
where the window opened out

to one half-shed sycamore,
two spruce, an open field,

and a tree line at dusk
that fenced in all the things

we knew names of, and beyond it
lay all the things yet without names,

the way time stretches over
the clean, black surface of water,

and the glasses were full
of whiskey, and a banjo twanged

on the car radio
as the road wound up

out of this dead city, over the hill,
into the quiet dark beyond

a future we didn't even worry about
trying to know.

Between Times

I looked long between the times
you were not here and the times

when you would be here again,
to find only a whole star's worth of light

and the river water's receding
into the sacred dark of sleep

where music notes softened and fell
the way rain filled the bedroom

that morning when you were here
before you were not,

when all that was left in the waiting
was the sparrow's song stretching new

year's light farther out beyond where it touched
the empty hands of the wind and folded over

the sound of the distance between
the last leaf and the sky.

Reconciliation

In St. Joseph's Cathedral when the priest was preaching,
There is no sin for which God will not forgive,

under the high dome of ascending angels
and outstretched arms of the savior,

flat profiled faces of shepherds
collecting the blood of the lamb,

all backgrounded by pastel blue-green afterlife skies,
all I could think of was how that one Sunday evening

in the morning of our marriage, you enveloped me
until I was barely able to open my eyes to see

the pastel blue-green butterfly tattoo
on the small of your back lifting and falling,

lifting and falling, like the dolphins you chased
along the shore once after we'd shared a joint

in the beach-house laundry room,
how they semi-circled through the evening surf,

surfacing, descending, surfacing,
the sky a dome of pastel blue green.

From the house-deck I watched you, your figure,
shrinking, awkwardly sand-striding northward,

folds of your skirt trailing and flippering,
camera clutched in one hand, desperately

trying to capture still, what maybe you realized
was purity, and, by then, was drifting

farther and farther
out of reach.

Directional

West, where
you came up
from the river
even more beautiful
than the orange red
of the dying day.

East, where
all children imagine
worlds beyond
their knowing
dawning.

Here, where
you cannot see
the river,
but you know
it is there, just beyond
the trees, footing the hills,

as sure as you know
a vein lies
under skin,

a voice waits
behind closed lips,

thousands
of invisible years
envelop the life of a stone
worn by that same river
you cannot see,

the sound
of the baby's cry lingers
between her silent sleeping
and the few still seconds
before her waking,

a seed-star
hides inside every apple
just as my mother showed me
when I was five,

and the water
in the river is
moving
was moving
will move
rock and stone
and dirt and mud
and love.

South, where
the universe expands
beyond our seeing
beyond our knowing
beyond
light and dust and dark.

North, where
your love is a window
locked against winter,
or an apple, unpicked,
your star, waiting.

All We Live Through

Remember the way the sky bled the first time
into that night and moon brightening the fruit
trees' fruits hanging low and pulling toward the ground
even then already skin-browned with time and rot.

Remember how the hills above the town
enwrapped rivers and rust and ruins
and lives lived and over before beginning,
the boys who fell over dead or put guns to their heads
or swung themselves from their necks
in the backyard where their sisters came home
to find them suspended there in the evening,
endings started with loving, restarted with dying.

Remember all you ever knew
heaped into the corner of the room down the hall,
a conversation through walls turning the story
all wrong, from love to rage to guts ripped and strewn,
bodies finally cleared from the stage, all the players' lines
spoken, bereft of direction, staring silent
into the wide black fourth-wall void to where
the tide was folding and unfolding the light,
dying and undying toward a new taste at last.

Remember the leavening, honey and breath and heat,
a heart pounding, skin ripening, and finally
numbed sleep at the water's edge, a mirrored face,
a blank page where all the words still unwritten pull
and push from womb and blood and ash and everything
that follows after all we lived through—now the unbreaking,
now the first touching, now the awakening within
the currents of morning, dawning soft and red and new.

Not the Same Red

What we now call
love is not

the same as what
we then called love,

not the same red
that once colored

the bedsheet curtain
tinting the room dark

auburn backlit by midwinter
afternoon sun,

and I slumping broken against
the wall, and down

the hall no windows,
barely any light at all

but what could travel
toward the cracked

and empty porcelain tub
to catch the all the blood.

*
What we now call
love is not

the same as what
we then called love,

not the same red
as her flushed cheeks

and green bridesmaid's dress
as she rode in the passenger seat

up Rt. 40 drunk beyond midnight
with one hand up

her dress and her other
clutching mine.

*
What we now call
love is not

the same as what
we then called love,

not the red of thirty
years ago in summer

afternoons of flushed red
flesh and hot breath

and no knowledge of anything
beyond the immediate

nearly unbearable new
sensation of touch

and no parents home
for another two hours.

*

What we now call
love is different

shades of red, the deep red
of birth and everything after,

the shadow of far-off memories
and conceptions, and the red

hat she wore the moment you knew
she would be forever, fire-red

and flowering through winter's ice,
dusk-red over the valley, embers and smoke,

red rekindled from faded longing reborn
in rising and dying light,

half-shadowed and warmed by the red
that follows the first fall,

first cut, first pulse, first cry.

A Winter of First Wanting

Lying in the dim yellow of new morning
he watches his wife dressing

and in the mirror how she measures
her aging figure against the past,

running her fingertips across the scar spanning her belly,
and he remembers a long time ago, now,

when their new longing began turning the world back
into a place they could almost stand again, well before

they had paid any price, well before
anything near-death had scarred her white-smooth skin,

when they were a solitary two, folded every morning
into new time, new snow, new light.

He knows now, these wounds grip her longing still
beyond any returning to that one unscarred winter.

She studies them. She buries them,
each new morning in the dawn,

unaware of his silent adorations,
unaware of how the curves of her side,

the bare small of her back,
veiled in the milky coming on of new light,

will never fail to bring his longing back
to that winter of first wanting,

back beyond any new shape, any new wound,
back before they knew anything about anything at all.

IV.

. . . it is a serious thing
just to be alive
on this fresh morning
in the broken world.

~Mary Oliver

Waiting for My Son

I. Sighting

North on the old right of way
the dog pulls toward each new scent—
white tail, woodchuck, river-smell.

At Pike Island damn
the river that cut this valley
slips by in silent currents.
Bare branches tangle
against ribbons of cloud.

Pausing there above the river
below the sky
I wait for you,
still three months gestating,
only now the size of a small fist
cocooned against the world.

A bald eagle circles northward.

II. Distance

A mother purple finch
nests in a basket of impatiens.
Centered in pink,
four blue eggs—wings waiting.

Across the Ohio
the sun drops behind the western hill,
and the mother finch has grown impatient

with my presence,
and I, more impatient to meet you.

The distance between here
and the only house on the left
is not far—
you will learn the way east up Cherry Hill,
south along Table Rock Lane,
and then GC&P road
where I nearly fell to death
in a dream once
when I was only six years old.

III. Presence

Today, I read poems on the porch
while the sun broke
over the eastern hill,
the dog lazed,
and we waited for you
to fill the empty morning
with your beating heart
your breath, your voice,
your cry.

You have no choice,
you will inherit this place.
It becomes who you are,
you become what it is—

river and rock,
hill and tree,
field and ridge.
And everything beyond
around here
is what you're not.

IV. Girty's Point

Cresting a ridge on Stone and Shannon Road,
I thought of you, still enwombed,
nearly ready to enter
this great stage of fools.

Above the Ohio,
eye-level with a circling hawk,
I stop in the silence, waiting
for breath to come easy again.
Way below, the river snakes
down from Brilliant toward Wheeling
and then on, and on still.

Near Girty's Point I paused
to watch a thunderstorm
push its way through the river valley.

Here, out in the large unknown
room of the universe,
never outside of anything,
we are always within,
earth, and sky, and time.

V. Home

The finches have hatched
and already fled.
But now you are finally here.
You are home.
Swaddled, sleeping, still,
awaiting your awakening
to the world.

One day we will walk to the river.
You will touch the water,
feel the dirt and the mud,
I will teach you the meaning of *Ohio,*
and you will look across currents
to the western hills,
in silent wonder,
and begin your knowing, then.

The Unfolding

Tonight, trying to comfort my son
from what he now accepts as real death,

I think of how I used to lie in my boyhood bed
staring through near sleep up and out the window,

between tangled branches shuddering in the wind,
the winter moon, the milky-blue night sky,

listening above my own fears, miles away down in the valley,
to the currents of the Ohio unfolding and unfolding and unfolding.

Now mourning for all those he knows
he will one day lose, he climbs, sobbing, up into our bed,

burrowing into his mother's arms as close as physics will allow,
and I know what he is trying to do, where he is trying to go.

Folded now, deep within the rhythms of her voice,
he falls to sleep, and in that sleep, they embrace

so completely, trying to hold each other back
from what they both know will dawn only hours from now,

trying both to go back to what they once were—
with him, alive inside, sleeping, waiting,

everyday listening to the rhythm of her heart,
the notes of the songs she hums to him,

the pulse of her blood feeding him
tucked safe within that dark space of beginning,

where no knowledge can enter of mourning and age and pain,
only blood, and water, and mother, and persistent time,

ushering him closer and closer toward entering
the currents of his own life,

toward entering his own
unfolding.

Drop-Off and Pickup

I sit behind my father after he picks me up from school, my little arms clenched to his sides as he guides his red Suzuki motorcycle north on GC&P Road, turning and bending with the shape of the waters of Long Run. It is late September, warm and bright, and the road snakes and inclines into the hills toward home. I am tired from a whole day of learning the alphabet and counting to new numbers. I drift off to sleep, tiny hands falling in dead weight from the sides of my father.

I dream of water and sun and the leaves of the tree canopy above, filtering the light down into the creek, clear and untainted, running pure and clean down out of the hills toward Wheeling Creek, and from there on into the Ohio.

Suddenly, there is a voice, my father yelling my name, shaking me awake where he had pulled to the side of the road once he had felt my arms go slack. My head snaps upright from where it fell to my shoulder into the dream of water and sun and leaves.

*

Every day when I drop my son off at school I think about death. Either his or mine. Either today, or in some far-off future. I wonder how he would process the events of my death if it happened today. I wonder if he will remember, later in life, our daily ritual for drop-off in front of the school—a sequence of four different fist bumps, and then a high-five handshake and bro hug, and then I always say, *Guess what?*

He says, *What?*

I love you, I say.

Silence.

Did you hear me, buddy boy?

Yeah, he says, and I can feel him pulling away, and then he's off and running toward the doors of the school, my voice following him, *Try your best.* He turns and gives a thumbs up.

I'm proud of you, I say, but he's beyond earshot.

And then he's gone, through the door and into the confines of the school. Every day since pre-school we do this, and almost every day I think about how it could be the last time we ever see each other. I have to sit there in the van before driving off to work, trying to contain my fear, to make myself stop imagining, holding back this inexplicable power of blood-love, hating that we live in a world where a father has to feel this, a world where schools are places where children get shot. Almost every day I think about Sandy Hook, what it must have looked like, all those little bodies bloodied on the floor, all that suffering. I guess their God thought all those parents were strong enough to handle it. What was God going to do with all those prayers sent after their little boy was gunned down, after their beautiful girl's life ended in a moment of chaos and terror?

*

I'm watching my father struggle through old age. I wonder more often now about that day on the motorcycle after pickup from kindergarten.

What if I had fallen? What if I had died? Where would he be right now? Would he even be alive? Would he be himself? Could he have even gone on?

*

I saw on the news a flag-draped coffin, the arms of a twelve-year-old boy wrapped around it. His soldier-father must have been sent to war, handed a gun to shoot at other men with guns in another country. He hugs the casket and won't let go. People are telling him he has to, but he doesn't move, his whole body nearly draped over the casket blanket-like, arms spread wide as if he wants to pick it up and carry it away, his cheek pressed hard against the lid as if listening for his father to tell him one last time something that might help him make sense of the world. I think of them a long time—the twelve years the boy had with his father, what they probably did, how he probably loved him without even knowing why or how immeasurable a boy's love for his father can be, how they maybe threw ball, wrestled in the living room, watched their favorite baseball team, talked about silly stuff, talked about serious stuff. I can't shake it—boy and coffin and grief—the permanence of the longing that follows loss.

*

Once, after pickup from school, I heard my son's six-year-old voice from the back seat of the car: *Daddy, how will I keep being myself when you die?*

*

At the end of the school day, I stand around with the other parents. We wait for our sons and daughters to be let back into the world where it's up to us again to keep them safe, up to us to keep them from dying before we do, up to us, at the very least, to show them how much beauty and love is in the world if they learn how to look for it, how to notice it. I think that's why I'm always pointing out to my son the changes in the hills, the rhythms of the river—new snow clinging to branches, yellow-green buds beginning to form just overnight, so many shades of green in midsummer, the churning of a barge upriver, a train whistle from the west bank. If he knows where to look and how to listen, maybe he won't enter each day with the same imaginings that anchor my fears—a classroom sprayed with bullets, little boys and girls in pools of blood, their lives gone just like that, in a glimmer and flash of time that both moves and stands still.

*

I know just beyond the trees the river is moving. It is late September, warm and bright, and I'm guiding the car through the valley toward home, my son in the backseat after pickup looking out the window up at the hills. I remember the dream, the clear creek water running, the canopy of leaves filtering the sun, my father calling my name.

At a stop light I look up into the hills, too, not for any kind of sign, but searching for the beauty that can help temper this fear, accepting the truth of that paternal pull of blood and time, the truth that everything after this moment, this second, belongs to the unknown, the truth that every day I'm trying so hard to let my son go, and, in the same moment, to save him from dying.

Van Gogh's Sky

Thank God my mother
never said anything about heaven
when she pointed up, showing me
for the first time, Orion,
hanging low in late autumn,
just cresting the eastern hill.

Tonight, it is my son pointing upward,
and I'm tempted to tell him
how the Kiowa believe
the stars of the Big Dipper
were seven sisters running in fear
from their bear brother
and suddenly borne up into the sky,

or how the Blackfoot believe
the stars of the Pleiades
were seven orphan brothers
who could not stand the world
and wanted only to play
and so were suddenly turned
into light and dust.

But his awe writes its own myth
on into the whirling yellow stars
awash around a golden moon,
in tonight's black-blue sky that he
tells me looks just like Van Gogh's.

I want him to promise
to remember this one day,

standing under the open sky,
holding his father's hand,
years from now,
after tasting sweet ripe fruits,
and the bitterness of mourning,
once truth has broken through,
with all its agony and joy,
wheeling like the stars
one after another,
each second on into the next.

Full Count

Under the shadow of the coal
conveyor at Benwood,
my son takes the mound
one out away from
the Mountaineer Little League
World Series title.

    Ball one, low.

Late summer evening,
the river still slipping by,
I watch his young body,
tall and strong and lean,
as he checks the runner at first
and then glides into the stretch.

    Strike one, looking.

He kicks the dirt by the rubber,
gets his footing and balance,
adjusts his cap, stares down the batter.

    Ball two, outside.

The sun sets early in the valley,
the ballfield lights flicker on,
you'd think the scene
worthy of the silver screen.
And the pitch.

    Ball three, outside.

He is beautiful. He is a poem.
He kicks his knee high,
strides out across the mound,
arm reaches back with the ball,
delivers, and paints the black
on the outside corner.

      Strike two, swinging.

I take a breath, tell myself
to remember this, always,
remind myself my life is now
over half over.

      Full count.

Under the long late-summer shadows
across the outfield, and in between,
the sun, and all the unseen,
he still has everything left to love,
left to win, and left to lose.

      Foul tip. Full count.

Fearless, he likes the inside
fast ball call from the catcher,
nods his head, enters the stretch,
knee kicks up, leg strides out,
torso uncoils, left arm slings
an arrow toward home . . .

Little Blue Box

I can't remember how to breathe so the nurse hands me a brown paper bag along with the white jumpsuit and matching cap. Sixty seconds before that they wheeled my wife away, her belly bulging under the white blankets, in her belly, our baby choking. Sixty seconds before that, the room a flurry of nurses and someone saying, *We have to take the baby,* like there's a place where they take babies and never bring them back. Sixty seconds before that the baby's heart rate crashing and the pulsing alarm. Sixty seconds before that joking that I hope the baby gets born fast so I don't miss the golf on TV later. That was four minutes ago. Four minutes ago, everything was normal. Four minutes ago, I assumed everything would happen as it did when my son was born. But this is different. This time I'm hyperventilating, thinking I may never see my wife again, thinking our baby girl might die, the nurse smiling, patting me on the back, saying how they always seem to forget the dads in these situations. It's not funny, but she tries to be. Nothing about this is funny. My baby girl is choking. And this is real. And she could die. And we don't know which way to spell her name. And I can't remember how to breathe.

*

The baby won't eat. She spent her whole first day of life throwing up breast milk and bottle milk, and she's not the right color so they've put her in a little plastic box of blue light with four holes, two on each side, so that we can reach in and touch her. She doesn't move much. She seems so tired. She just lies there really still on her back, her eyes covered with a little baby sleep mask to keep out the blue light. I can see her tiny belly going up and down. My wife hasn't come to the nursery yet. They cut the baby out and she is in pain, but I don't think that pain is what's keeping her away. I know better than to try to understand.

*

The baby won't eat. They've put a tube up her nose and down her throat so she gets nourishment. I sit here for long stretches of time talking to her while she lies in her little blue box. I talk to her about her mom, her big brother, and her grandparents, and the only house on the left where I grew up with her aunt and uncle, and our big St. Bernard dogs, and the tall spruce and Osage and apple and maple trees and the woods and green fields. I tell her about how in winter on a clear day you can hike up the southern hill all the way to the top to where the trees clear just at the crest and look out over the open field down toward the valley, and if you time it just right, you can watch the lowering sun turn the snow and the brown seed heads in the field to a hundred different shades of orange and gold before it finally settles behind the hills and is gone.

*

I am watching my wife hold the baby. It was awkward for the nurse, the tangle of tubes and wires, lifting her up out of the little blue box. In the rocking chair my wife gives a speech to the baby about how she has to be strong because that is what all the women in her family do. I know for a fact that this is true. I've seen it. No matter what, they took care of everything. While their men went off to mine coal or to fight in wars or to mold steel, the women held it all together with their hands and their wills, always, and never complained. They're strong. They don't give in, ever.

*

I am holding on to my big sister and can't let go. I can't breathe again, and I haven't slept. They told us they are taking the baby again. She's been losing weight, even with the tube shoved up her nose and down her throat, and they're all too stupid here to be able to help her. I don't want to be here, so I keep holding on to my sister.

I want to go back to when I was five and she was ten and it was summer, and the trees were so green, and we rode bikes and made up stupid songs and names and she dressed me up to play a flower girl in her pretend wedding. Or when she dressed me up as Horton the Elephant and tried to tape big construction paper cut-out ears and a trunk on my head. But we're not there and then. We're here and now, and this is happening.

*

I know to go north, but I'm not paying attention to the road. At each bump my wife winces in the passenger seat because it was only four days ago when they cut her open. We don't talk. We have no idea what to say. In mid-March everything is dormant and dark. I'm tired of everything being dead and brown and gray, the color of ash or closed-down factories or the smoke from the stacks along the river. Even the trees are gray and dark, ticking past like seconds on a clock, only faster than seconds. Somewhere ahead of us the baby is in her little blue box in the back of an emergency medical transport. I don't know how fast I'm going but I know I'm on Highway 22 moving in the general direction of Pittsburgh.

*

From a high room with a big window and a Giraffe intensive care unit in the middle, another flurry of nurses, and one says, *We need your permission,* and I think, what am I supposed to say? I can't talk or think. *Sir, we need your permission,* she says, and I say, *What will happen?* and she says, *The baby will die,* so we say, *Yes, yes, God, yes,* and in the background they're trying to find a vein for the IV, but there are hardly any places left for needles, and the baby is screaming louder now than she has in all her four days and eleven hours. And there's pain and confusion but everyone seems calm with urgency. And I'm watching all of this from the corner of the room and can't do anything about any of it, thinking that every minute people either end up dying or keep on not dying.

*

Everyone is gone, just me and my new baby girl, and night coming on and the quiet calm in the room, except for the click click click of the pump pushing in more blood every so often. Through the raindrops on the huge window by the ledge where I'm sitting, I see Pittsburgh all spread out below, the sky growing darker, and the city lights lighting up until backed by the full black sky. From way up here on the whatever floor, the city fully lit now in tiny lights, everything looks all held together in webs of bridges and rivers and traffic pulsing through, lights reflecting in the water. When the traffic files in at intersections, and the signals turn red to green, all the lights start moving, floating across the bridges over the rivers that mirror the city, this way toward my window high above, little perfect pairs of diamonds, gliding over the water, brighter and closer and brighter and closer, until they're almost blinding, until I'm almost not even thinking, until I'm not even trying to remember how to breathe.

Someone Else's Blood

I. Above St. Mary's

Outside your hospital window
tombstones loom above the bones
of the long-buried with the silence
of memory and sleep.

Inside, you are so close
to not living,
connected, wired, injected,
lying in a little plastic box,
enwombed in blue light.

Every three hours I prop you up,
cup your tiny head in my palm,
stare at your battered little face,
tilt a bottle to your mouth—
white dribbles over reddened and purpled flesh.

You barely open your eyes,
barely ask for anything,
I wonder if you even asked for this,
for this life, for this birth,
into all this sorrow and dreaming,
into all this fight and hurt.

II. Circulation

When they handed me all three pounds of you,
we did not know then
that our blood was, somehow, not enough.

We did not know then,
the tubes and coils of wires, still,
and inside moving fluid keeping you fed.

We did not know then,
your tiny arms, too bruised and needle holed.

We did not know then,
the volume of your cries
while they stuck the needle
over and over and finally
straight into your belly.

Then we knew we were moving,
but not through time, somehow.
Somehow the laws of physics changed.
Somehow in this, everything stopped,
nothing circulated, no blood, no time,
and you were everything—needle and pulse and oxygen.

On Highway 22 East outside of Pittsburgh
we are not moving with time
but knowing names of objects
framed through the windows:
trees, stream, sky, building, car, rain.

Each drop on the windshield
is a universe of time wiped away,
and in a half-second, resurrected.

And then we are with you again.
You're too sad and beautiful to look at.

Out the hospital window,
beyond the cemetery
and down across Lawrenceville's evening lights,
the 40th Street Bridge conveys traffic
across the Allegheny,
living people in real time
moving through space
over water, on land, on a planet,
around a star,
in a moving universe.

III. Transfused

Evening turns to night,
I sit beside you
watching someone else's blood
slowly pump into you.

It is a stream, a clock, our time.

A body is a clock.
Blood is river is a clock.

I give thanks
to dogs from the 17th century,
to William Harvey,
to Richard Lower,
to the human intellect,
to the human will.

I think maybe now you'll live
long enough for me to show you
how the universe keeps time
in the last three orange leaves
on a black branch,
in a snow-crusted creek bed at dawn,

in yellow-green mornings,
in the orange evening sun slanting
through pine-boughs,
and in the currents of the river
that will never stop unfolding
with your new pulse, your new breath,
your new blood.

A Blossom

> *There are days we live*
> *as if death were nowhere*
> *in the background*
> ~Li-Young Lee

Since you nearly died
after only three days,
I cannot think of the dawn
and not think of you
in the same light,
or of a blossom newly bursting,
dogwood pink, redbud purple,
or cherry white,
blooming into its own age,
its moment of ripening,
its final silent
flittering descent.

Something so weightless,
even has weight.

Like your tiny hand
on mine,
soft and heavy
as a petal flipping
through spring wind.

Since you nearly died after
only three days,
I'm okay
with not knowing.

I'm okay
with the unanswered,
with giving everything,
as a blossom offers up
all its weightlessness.
And I'm okay
that meaning can be
as lucid as water,
or as complex as your eyes
reflecting back into mine
a blueness shared by blood,
or as certain as the light
of each dawn
bringing one less day,
one less moment,
one more blossom,
opening, ripening,
and falling.

Whiskey and the Universe

We each start with blank white space,
with you in the next room

painting a world all your own and
me in here drinking whiskey and writing poems,

turning the tree outside the window
into an infinite universe of flowering

and shedding and flowering, and no matter
when, blackbirds huddle in the branches,

each onyx eye reflecting the convex turn
of distance and time when you were

in there and I was in here drinking whiskey and
writing poems about loving you even more

because the tree outside the window
filled with blossoms and birds and

kept our time in its branches as sure as
a stone sheds its shape in rushing water

and now you're in the next room painting and
I'm in here drinking whiskey and writing poems

because I put you in this world, on this page,
and because it's never quite as simple as

a black bird on a bare black branch,
a worn stone in a clear stream,

choosing which color should come next,
which word should follow this one.

Still Alive, Still Signing

    for Allison Bertozzi (1992—2017)

On the morning of the day
I heard that Alli died,
I also learned that before
his mind was erased by time,
my wife's grandfather would wake
every morning, pack his pail,
and leave for the mine
in the five o'clock dark, returning
coal-dusted by five in the evening
and tend to his orchard,
the apple, pear, plum,
and peach, trees all in neat rows
in blossom in the spring,
branches weighted full in autumn.

I pictured him there in the garden
walking the rows sampling
the fruit of the seeds
his own hands had buried,
bringing to his wife
his life's harvest,
how it must have tasted
after all day digging
in a coal seam,
sharp and sweet,
like brand new light.

*

In the afternoon of the day
I heard that Alli died
I learned the doctor told
my father there was nothing left
he could do for him,
that he had made his own pain
with his own life,
and it was now,
and real, and final,
and finally, all his own.

*

And later, it was evening
on Hess Avenue,
an hour after
I heard that Alli died,
and I witnessed my own daughter
with her tiny five-year-old hands
shaping small figures
from Play Doh,
singing to herself
as she sculpted each one to life,
and I began to fashion
fictions for each of them.

The one shaped from black clay
worked his life away
in a coal mine,
but when he was not underground,

he harvested loads upon loads
of picked fruit
for the woman he loved,
and he never until his dying day
forgot who she was.

The blue clay figure was a father,
and he ran for miles and miles
over the hills, down into the valleys,
never once losing his legs,
never once losing his hands,
never once losing his dignity.

And the bright purple clay figure
I named Allison, and she was beautiful
and young, with a whole brand-new life
shaped from my daughter's hands,
born out of my wishing
the real world away,
and I gave her a story
that went on and on and on,
so her mother and father would
never have to enter into this mourning.

*

I sipped the gin from my glass,
breathed in the juniper and lime,
instructed myself to feel

for the earth rolling underneath,
the hills rising to cover the sun,
to remember the truth
that light never really leaves the sky,
to listen for the evening chorus of the living—

the thrush high in the Elm branches,
the quiet lapping of the river below,
the sound of my own daughter,
still alive, still singing.

March Morning, 2020

A sparrow lights on the rain gutter,
fills the hollow sound of winter with an ancient song.

Empty branches on the west side
of the hill await a late winter snow.

It is so cold. The house is a wreck,
last night's dishes need done,

my daughter's paintings lie strewn
across the living room floor.

The coalfields have come even closer
overnight. And a virus is spreading.

Families sleep apart, mothers and fathers gone
to wars we keep fighting but have forgotten why.

Loved ones can only wave to the dying
from behind the glass.

Below the underpass on the banks of Wheeling Creek
the homeless huddle against their own lost lives.

But it's okay here. The kids and wife are asleep
upstairs under warm weighted quilts,

the dogs curled in beside them,
and the whole world gone remote.

When they wake, I want to tell them I'm here,
my life is theirs, their lives are everything.

Not quite yet light. And a virus is spreading.
But it's all okay. Dawn is just coming on,

up the hill at the only house on the left, the cardinals
and finches will be gathering at the feeder,

we have the whole day ahead, and everything
will be back to normal soon.

Father-Daughter Discussion

I. Things My Nine-Year-Old Daughter Said on the Way to School After Watching the Russian Bombing of Ukraine on the Morning News

*Dad, so many people got killed, and three children,
three children, Dad.*

*Why don't they just get all the Ukraine
people on a plane and get them out of there?*

*Were there ever any wars
in our country, Dad?*

Why did people have slaves?

*Wait, we fought against England
but now we're on their side?*

*I think George Washington
was our best President.*

*Did they ever catch that guy
that killed Abraham Lincoln?*

Ugh, I can't stand that Russia president.

*During Black Lives Matter, didn't the white people know
what Martha Luther King, Jr. said?*

*Dad, so many people got killed, and three children,
three kids, Dad.*

*If I were rich and had a plane,
I would go over there and just get them all out.*

*What can we do? We need to do something, Dad,
to help them. What should we do, Dad?*

II. My Response

How do you answer
the unanswerable?
Tell her to hold a sign,
that we'll send some money,
write our congressman,
plan a protest,
turn off the tv,
tell her it is going to be okay?

Or tell her the truth?

Tell her that monsters are real,
that men have been killing each other
for the same reasons
for thousands and thousands of years.

I want to tell her
I don't have the answers,
that I have the same
questions she does.

So I say, *Learn. Learn
the names of the trees.*

*Take note how the sugar maple
turns its brilliant orange red,
the oak, its deep russet,
and the sycamore, its bright yellow.*

*Learn how to inhale the scent
of a perfect autumn afternoon,
and watch how the sun lights
the trees a-blaze as if they
themselves are slowly burning.*

*Learn the birds' names
from only their song,
and watch as the finches
and cardinals gather in the evening
at the feeder under the pear tree
that your great-grandfather planted.*

*This is the only way
not to hear the bombs
falling 5000 miles away,
not to see under wreckage
and rubble and billowing smoke
the suffering and loss and grief.*

*Learn what it means to live
in a world of light and dark.*

*Learn to praise,
and to give thanks,
and just to keep loving
the way your heart loves,*

and listen and look
and smell and breathe,
and know it's okay
to feel, to feel it all,
and let it all fill your heart,
already so aching,
already overflowing.

Finally, Ohio

With the last load of our lives
packed up and boxed into the van,
we turn south onto River Road,
past the 24th Street playground
where my daughter first learned
about falling and always getting back up,
past the Altmeyer funeral home,
the closed-down Rite-Aid,
Smith Oil, the shopping plaza,
and the Lock 12 ball field at 3rd Street
where my son came in for relief,
bases loaded, and sat down three batters in a row
in the Mountaineer Little League World Series,
past the rusted-out walls of Center Foundry,
and the tiny sign commemorating Chuck Howley,
beyond the Save-a-Lot and McDonalds
until the *Welcome to Warwood* sign
flashes in the side mirror,
and then we're gone,
on the open stretch of highway
into North Wheeling,
where dilapidated Victorian homes
line each side of Rt. 2,
then up the ramp onto I-70,
across the Fort Henry Bridge
while under us, the Great River glides on,
and once over Wheeling Island,
we begin the gentle climb into the hills,
up out of the crumbling valley
and into Belmont—beautiful mountain,

my son and daughter in the back seat,
their backs now against all those fifteen years
that we are driving away from,
all those milestones ticking by
like fence posts in the rearview—
first words, first crawls, first steps, first falls,
all the dated growth notches on the kitchen wall
painted over, the house ready for sale,
and the only thing in front of us
is finally a new life beyond the river,
finally, familial ground,
finally, Ohio.

Inventory

You wake up with blood in your piss,
and inventory the following:

> three bottles of pills,
> half a bottle of bourbon,
> one house,
> one wife (still),
> two children,
> two cars,
> two and half jobs,
> one bachelor's,
> one master's,
> one PhD,
> thousands upon thousands of dollars of debt,
> twenty-three rejections,
> zero publications,
> fifty extra pounds,
> and forty-two Weight Watchers points.

You reflect on the weight of the sum divided by its parts
equal to something greater than anything divisible by labels.

You remember once, when your daughter fit
perfectly in the bend of your arm, how small, how helpless.

You look at your son and remember
an afternoon on the riverbank skipping rocks into the wake.

You sit on the west-facing hill at the only house on the left,
where you don't know how much longer the living will live.

You listen to cicadas churring in late September,
smell the coming on of rot and leaf fall and early dark.

You take note of all the stars in the universe
that suddenly focus into perfect points of dust and light.

You think some things you just can't number,
some things are just beyond any need for counting.

Iron Man

. . . i hear
my ill-spirit sob in each blood cell . . .
                    ~Robert Lowell

One Saturday morning you see your vegan, teetotaling big brother as a little blip on a map in the Iron Man Triathlon app, tracking his whereabouts up to the second, and every now and then you check in on the updates—1mi of 2.4 mi left to swim, 56 mi of 112mi left to bike, 12mi of 26.22 mi left to run—just thinking of it makes you want to collapse into the moldering heap of your own never-accomplished goals.

Imagine how that induces reflection and self-conversation as you sit down in front of the television to dig into your fresh home-cooked breakfast—three over-medium eggs, three slices of thick-cut bacon, a mound of hash browns, sausage gravy, rye toast with butter, and a bloody mary from your own special recipe that you count as one of your finest life-achievements—and before you can fork your first bite of egg, the Iron Man app alert double chimes, telling you your brother has swum 3 miles in what you will learn later were the jellyfish-infested, 49-degree waters of the Chesapeake Bay, and has now biked 60 miles with only 52 left to go, and after that, only 26 miles left to run. You think of the significance of those same numbers—49, the number of years you have currently wasted. 60, the number of years you hope to live well beyond. 52, only two years and one-hundred-fifty-three days from now. 26, the age when you were last semi-attractive to women.

There is a line across which pride rolls itself into jealousy and spite.

Imagine how it feels, taking a bite of yolk-covered hash browns and bacon, washing it down with a gulp of double-Tito's spicy bloody mary, and knowing that if you listen hard enough, you can hear as one fat cell splits into another, puffed full of self-loathing and self-deprecation the very second they are born, knowing that you will bear them with you, along with all you have unachieved, every second that you trudge and slog closer and closer to your own finish line.

V.

How soon unaccountable I became tired and sick,
Till rising and gliding out I wander'd off by myself,
In the mystical moist night-air, and from time to time,
Look'd up in perfect silence at the stars.

~Walt Whitman

Conversation at Dawn

First, let's get the odd and uncomfortable
small talk out of the way.

In fact, let's just skip that part
all together and go big.

Let's not even talk at all for a while.
No need to fill the silence with senseless noise.

Let's just listen to what the morning
is saying in the songs of sparrows and starlings,

in the dawning pale-orange light
drying the last glassy beads of dew from the grass.

Let's just close our eyes for a minute, take a breath,
and let ourselves be held by the mountains and rivers.

Okay, now, tell me about you, the big things,
where you're from, what you believe,

what you hear and see in morning songs,
how the sky is always phasing into a shifting orange blue.

Tell me here, in the newness of this beginning.
I want to listen, to hear something good.

Tell me about the first time you saw
something so beautiful that it hurt.

Then, after a while, maybe you can listen to me.
But don't expect any answers, only questions.

Let me ask you how it is
I am so grateful and sorrowful all at once.

Let me ask you how it is
you cannot constantly be thinking about suffering.

Let me ask you if the riddle of the world
could be solved in this sacred communion of morning.

Let me ask you if you think
it matters, after all these thousands of years

that we have never thought
of a more accurate word for *sunrise*.

Now, You Are

Now,
you can't move,
can't walk, can't stand straight,
can't talk right, can't lift
the mug of soup to your mouth
or stab the slices of fresh summer
peach I brought and cut for you today.

Now,
you are gazing
out the window with nothing left
to wait for but winter and sleep.

Now,
you have just enough
strength left to lumber up the stairs
to cradle your newborn
grandson in your arms.

Now,
you are not in a wheelchair,
but sitting on the porch
laughing and telling stories.

Now,
you are leading us fearless
into the roaring and raging
sea, under a waving red flag.

Now,
by the rush
of the same blue sea at night,
the lights of a ship's beacon flash,
and we drink gin in the silence
of the steady hushed
language of land and water.

Now,
you are reading to me,
and I listen. My first language lessons:
Dear Hamlet, do not forever with thy vailed lids
Seek for thy noble father in the dust.

Now,
you are running the ridge
of Table Rock Lane,
with legs and arms and a heart
that all work.

Now,
you are walking,
and we follow you
into a wide field
filling with snow
between rows and rows of pines,
and we hear the teeth
of the sawblade cutting deep.

Now,
we trail waist-high behind
while you drag the fresh-cut Christmas spruce
through snow, branches swishing,
evening falling into soft gray and white,
across the field toward home.

Now,
you are holding me
in the icy water,
and I am clinging to you
with cold and fear.

Now,
you let me go,
and I am not
drowning but breathing.

Now,
I know
there is nothing
to be afraid of.

Now,
I know
that even always
comes to an end.

When Your Father Is Dying

After you get the call at work and learn they are stopping antibiotics and switching to morphine, after you hear 24 to 48 hours but maybe longer because everyone is different, after you nearly break down in your boss's office, after you somehow make it to the parking lot where you hope nobody can hear you inside your car wailing, you somehow finally get your shit together enough to drive.

After the elevator, after the fourth floor, after the doctor says, *It is up to God now,* after you translate *God* into Nature, Cosmos, Universe, after your body wills you through time and space, you crest the highest point of I-70 in Belmont County, your senses heighten and fine-tune the world into eyes and ears and nose and skin and mouth, into the shape of the crescent moon, ribbons of orange-red cloud underlit and silvered by the setting sun, the curls of your daughter's hair, the perfect curve of her chin, the wide bright blue of your son's eyes, the lavender-soft skin of your wife's neck where you bury your sobbing face, the sweet sting of whiskey, the sad notes of a song.

*

You remember the decades in the nursing home, only it was just a few weeks, every day, spoon-feeding your father ice cream or cutting his favorite sandwich into fork-sized pieces. You say, *No* when asked if you want to see a picture of the wound on his back that's exposed his tailbone. You can't fathom how your mother has the strength to deal with this. You collapse wailing on the basement floor during your workout at 6am.

You take a break from the hospital room once a day and walk down the hall, stare out the fourth-floor window, across the parking lot and into the trees of the hills beyond thinking, *When will this ever end?*

You hold on to your sister so hard, wondering *What the hell would I do without her?* You gather around to watch the ballgame, hold the computer screen close while he tries to gather the strength to open his eyes and see the touchdown on replay.

You resist the memory of twenty-five years of never missing a gameday Saturday. You break down with your sister in the fourth-floor corner waiting room, knowing you'll never have a Saturday with your father again. You realize you've been mourning for days someone who is still living. You tell him you'll see him tomorrow and watch his slightest head nod.

You know he knows.

*

You arrive in the morning and notice the nurses jacked up the morphine overnight. You don't know your father is only twenty minutes from dying. You sit by the bedside and listen to his breathing, strained, labored. You hold onto his hand for the first time since you were a boy. Your sister arrives, thank God.

You both tell him you are there, and he manages another slight head nod. You tell him you love him. You tell him he doesn't have to feel any regret. You tell him you had the best childhood. You tell him Fuck Michigan, and your sister laughs through her tears. You feel death arrive in the room. You know this is it.

You clench his right hand. Your sister holds on to his left. You think how all he wanted six weeks ago was just to be outside again, see the sky, feel the sun, hear a birdsong. You watch him breathe, then stop, then breathe, then stop, then breathe, then stop. You see his eyes snap open for the first time in days, for the last time ever. You see him staring up into the void, searching beyond the ceiling for just one glimpse of clear blue sky.

You feel it happening. You watch his final breath. You sense, deep in the sudden stillness that follows the last exhale, a weight in the room lifting. You feel silence and time converge, and you are awash under waves of grief and peace.

*

You find your way across the sand to the edge of the sea holding your father's hand. You are still you, but you're a boy now. Your father is standing tall and walking you into the surge. You hear and feel and smell and taste the sea swell rolling in. You wade in against the cold, the salt, the wind, through the shallows further out, and further out still where the water wraps you in a womb of past and present. You feel the complete absence of half of who you are. You wonder what comes next, now that all the waiting is over?

You know your father is gone.

You stand waist-high in the swell under a crystal blue sky, a perfect orange sun rising. You look straight into the glittering calm just beyond the break-line. You hear on the shore behind, the ocean keeping time. You pull in your own breath deep. You exhale the weight of a thousand memories.

You let go of your father's hand.

Afterward

You enter the afterward
with an emptiness
as complete as any
one ending,
the first time
stepping on to the porch,
into the back yard,
with nothing to give meaning
to any one object,
to sparrow, and grackle,
to maple, and oak,
no word, no sound,
the feeders hanging empty
in the front garden,
the blue bird gone
from the fencepost house,
the nuthatch fled
from its branch
into the blinding
absence of everything,
time re-enveloping
like a womb
and your only wanting
is to forget
the end
and to be born
into everything else
before the dying started,
before everything else
was gone.

Leaving Home

I'd like to go now, and leave behind
all of this for someone else to deal with,

> the dishes in the sink, leftover breakfast on the stove, the constant pile of laundry, kitchen calendar filled with appointments and games and practices, pills on the windowsill, office desk with stacks of things, vehicle registration renewal, late math homework and book reports, lecture notecards and stacks of novels, drafts of poems I hate and will never finish, plaques on the wall, grass that needs mowing, dogs that need walking, mouths that need feeding . . .

but mostly I'd like to go and leave behind
the constant grip of the hand of grief

that seizes from inside in an instant,
the heaviness, the pounds,

the ocean daydreams, the crippling
reflections, the deathbed visions,

all these tributaries of mourning
feeding the gravity of the heart.

I'd like to go now and leave it all
and just wander off,

drift into some small town by a small river
and sit there on its banks in the sun,

watch its silent constant journey to some greater
body, always moving on, but never not there,

stillness and movement at once, like a man
confined to a deathbed, his body become

motionless, his words silenced by the morphine,
his mind flowing back over his years,

currents of happiness and sublime,
a wake of regret and grief.

If I get up and cross the river, will I
find any answers, will I find anything at all?

Father, is there even a chance
I will find you there?

Rt. 7 Confession

From the passenger seat I confess
all my failures and frauds,
how my teaching literature is a big act,
how I just get up there and pretend to be smart
and well-read and put on a show,
how calling myself a poet is a big lie,
how I hate every line I have ever written,
how everything now has no direction,
how I have no desire to do anything anymore.

Toward the off-ramp into Bridgeport
the too-familiar landmarks tick by—
Hanover Street intersection,
the condemned Aetnaville Bridge
spanning the dark back channel to Wheeling Island,
the burned-out shell of the Wilson Furniture building,
Moore's Music Emporium, now closed down
where over twenty-five years ago
I took guitar for a year during a pre-mid-life crisis.
(Good God, how old does that make me now?)

The entire drive snaking along the river's triggering towns,
and I can't help thinking how this whole valley has a way
of dropping an anchor into right your soul,
and I can't help from silently reciting
the haunted lines of James Wright:

> *For the river at Wheeling, West Virginia,*
> *Has only two shores:*
> *The one in hell, the other*
> *In Bridgeport, Ohio.*

And nobody would commit suicide, only
To find beyond death
Bridgeport, Ohio.

My writer's envy rages over how he wrote
words that meant something to people,
of his escape from this sad valley,
how nothing I write will ever matter as much,
how it's four months gone since I lost myself,
four months gone since I could write a single word.

Sometimes I hate this place so much,
crammed in houses on the hills,
cinder and salt winters,
mountains of bare-black trees,
Confederate flags on porches,
MAGA and Let's Go Brandon
in every other front yard,
rubber testicles hanging
from jacked-up pick-ups,
crumbling streets and brick buildings,
and panhandlers at the offramps
telling us that anything helps, God bless,
and myself, and so much more.

West on I-70 out of the valley
away from the river,
into the hills of Belmont County,
farther and farther into entropy,
and even in this winter dark
I know the day will dawn

slate-gray and dormant,
the dead will stay dead,
and I will never be any closer
to getting out of this place,
never closer to answering
any of the questions
the living keep living every day.

Winter Solstice Eve Morning

Today, eleven weeks to the day since
I felt my father's life fade away

into that undiscovered country,
the long riddle of his pain now solved with sleep,

a perfect silver waning crescent moon hangs,
white glowing in the pre-dawn, south-east sky,

its old, shadowed body perfectly visible
above this snow-dusted morning.

How is it we are always waxing,
always waning, always wandering

from light to shadow, shadow to light,
waiting for any kind of something more to emerge?

The grieving heart, too,
wanes and waxes like a moon,

waxing toward abundance,
waning toward emptiness,

from full and overflowing,
toward empty and broken.

Tomorrow, the darkest evening of the year,
while the solstice moon's waning light

emerges in the gloaming, I will kindle a fire,
I will drink a glass or three of whiskey,

I will breathe the first breath of winter,
I will look up through barren branches

and beyond, and when my wondering gazing crosses
the veil from here into the far end of possibility,

I will say a remembrance to my father,
I will watch the fire fade to embers,

the embers smolder to ash,
I will search whatever is left

in the newborn winter's night sky,
for any moon, any star,

any sign of any light,
any kind of something more than this.

Valley Pastoral: The View from Table Rock Lane, Election Day, 2024

Tucked into the valley, nearly out of sight,
the Ohio shore near Brilliant, Steubenville, and Weirton,
teems with the burning stench of Sulphur from Follansbee,
and up into the hills from rusting ruins
of Wheeling Steel in Beech Bottom,
the dark gray mounds and black slurry
of Tunnel Ridge Mine inch closer each day
to the top of Cherry Hill ridge.

But just beyond the edge of the sludge at the summit,
an ancient table-shaped sandstone monolith stands,
fixed in a cluster of oak, and maple, and locust,
on the old grounds of McCollough's Farm,
last fall's leaves half-rotted, some of this year's
still cling in orange, and red, and yellow,
a rake leans, solitary, on a mossy split-rail,
and life in the flowerbeds bends down
to the will of the wild and natural order of things.

From up here, way above the river,
where the billowing smokestacks seem to pillar the sky,
300 million years of natural history brushes across
the ancient surface of sandstone in the wind,
and in the half-shade half-sun
you can almost feel
some sense of hope in the days ahead,
and in the rustle and spiral of leaf-fall,
you can almost forget everything
we have lost,
for everything we have.

Daylight Savings Morning

I embrace the first frost,
5:24am, Autumn scent
of dry leaf-fall chill,
and the faint hint
of smoldering ash,
the dog nosing around
in the icy grass,
first perfect-black sky,
clear as glass,
Orion, like diamond pinpoints,
fixed in the deep black
dome of the unknown.

Over two years gone now,
long enough that your stories
are close to becoming myth,
long enough that your voice
echoes each time I ask
a question to the air
or see my reflection
and castigate myself
for never being good enough,
for being too overweight,
for too much drinking,
and still the vessel of grief
flows over into this season,
awash in color, in dying light,
in failing and fading and falling.

No wonder the maple leaf turns
such a brilliant red
just before its end,
no wonder that before
we knew what we know,
we thought what we thought
about the stars,
we painted on walls
patterns and pictures,
and pictures became words
and sacred light,
and then words turned
into stories,
and the stories into myth,
like the one about
the boy lost outside
in the early morning dark
who two years ago
gave his father to the stars,
and even though it was time
to turn time back,
he never gained
another hour,
never got back
another second.

Stars Without Stories

An urgency to learn the names of things arrives
as quickly as this morning's solitary hummingbird,
ruby-throated—*Archilochus colubris*—defying the strain of gravity,
wings beating fifty-three times in one second,
in each wingbeat, a lifetime, an evolution of stars
giving way to new light crossing into dawn,
and now the chorus of morning begins
with the piercing singular note
of the red-winged blackbird—*Agelaius phoeniceus*—melding
with the echoing call and response
of two northern cardinals—*Cardinalis cardinalis.*

After the hummingbird departs
I tally a roster of morning birds in attendance:
blue jay, tufted titmouse, American crow,
American robin, house sparrow, European starling,
House finch, red-shouldered hawk.
And the spring greenery: Japanese andromeda,
lily of the valley, fetterbush, mountain fire,
and I stifle the urge to look up
all their Latin equivalents.

I know that knowing the names of things
will not fill this hollowness of mourning,
nor will it make the things any more or less what they are,
any more or less beautiful, any more or less real,
the cardinal, any more or less its brilliant bright red,
but without names, while no less spectacular,
the constellations are just stars without stories.

I know this bird—*Zonotrichia albicollis*—is one
of thousands of white-throated sparrows,
and has lighted this morning on the branch
of *Pyrus Comminus*—the European pear tree,
whose white flowers are now bursting in rising sun.

Zonotrichia albicollis on a *Pyrus Comminus* branch,
no less than white-throated sparrow
in a European pear tree,
no less than all those names
and everything
reduced to this:

> brown bird sings on black
> branch, blooming white in morning,
> sweet balm for sorrow.

What We Have Left

This is what we have left
when everything else is gone—

clean smooth skin, the thought
of what was, the memory wet

and brown-blonde like the autumn dawn,
like your hair falling down on bare soft shoulders

that first summer on the mountain
above Uniontown, PA, and that evening,

quiet, still, but for birdsongs in the dusk,
clouds sealing up last sunlight on the skyline,

notes wrapping around warm
as the white shawl you wore,

the town glowing red orange
in the valley, our lives just begun,

and I remember remembering that February
evening driving up Market Street, while you

were just a little bit buzzy in your red turtleneck
and white winter hat, your face so young,

and you sang along to that cheesy love
song you love on the radio

*. . . the smile on your face lets me know that you need me.
There's a truth in your eyes saying you'll never leave me . . .*

and in that moment, I knew I knew there would
never be a time when I would ever not love you.

This is what we have left
when everything else is gone—

an ending, a beginning,
a song, our story, your voice,

my poem, and whatever
happens to come next.

Homecoming

In this new after-death
I've come back

to the only house on the left,
not knowing if I will

ever come back to life
at all

but here,
at least—

the wind in locust trees,
the shadow of youth,

the memory of this place
being everything,

scent of pine and sound of birdsong,
smell of spice and apples

just before the fall.

About the Author

W. Scott Hanna is a professor of English at West Liberty University, where he teaches creative writing and literature. His poetry and creative nonfiction have been published in *Pine Mountain Sand and Gravel, Cleaver Magazine, Still: The Journal, Porter House Review,* and others. He served as the poetry editor of the *Northern Appalachia Review* from its inaugural volume in 2020 until 2025. Born and raised in the Upper Ohio Valley, he currently lives in St. Clairsville, Ohio.

www.ingramcontent.com/pod-product-compliance
Lightning Source LLC
Chambersburg PA
CBHW022125160426
43197CB00009B/1154